DREAMLAND'S
BASIC
GENERAL SCIENCE
PART - 2

By

T. R. BHANOT

Published by

DREAMLAND PUBLICATIONS

J-128, KIRTI NAGAR, NEW DELHI - 110 015 (INDIA)
Tel : 011-2510 6050 Fax : 011-2543 8283
E-mail : dreamland@vsnl.com
www.dreamlandpublications.com

Published by
DREAMLAND PUBLICATIONS
J-128, Kirti Nagar, New Delhi - 110 015 (India)
Tel : 011-2510 6050, Fax : 011-2543 8283
E-mail : dreamland@vsnl.com
www.dreamlandpublications.com
ISBN 81-7301-404-3

Printed at :
Pearl Offset Press Pvt. Ltd

Preface

Life today is absolutely stamped with science. In order to live successfully in this **Science Age,** a scientific outlook is highly essential. Knowledge of at least the basic concepts of science is a must. This knowledge is sure to develop all-round scientific outlook, habits and attitudes. So, it goes without saying that the young minds should be given lessons in elementary science right from the beginning.

This book is the *second* volume on the subject of **GENERAL SCIENCE** and is meant for pupils of Form II.

The book comprises three units, each dealing with separate topics. The opening unit deals with the **Body and Its Upkeep.** In the second unit a child has been introduced to **Living and Non-Living Things** which it comes across so often. As for the natural environment, a beginner is supposed to be acquainted with the **Earth,** the **Moon,** the **Stars** and the **Seasons**. So, elementary facts about these aspects of nature have been covered in the closing unit.

The book conforms to the latest syllabus prescribed and released by the **NCERT** in the late 1990's. It has been written in a graded manner. Attractive four-colour illustrations and simple exercises with creative activity are some special features of the book.

I feel highly delighted while placing the book in the hands of teachers and the taught with a positive hope that it shall admirably fulfil their needs and create a place for itself by virtue of its plus-points.

— T. R. BHANOT

CONTENTS

THE LATEST SYLLABUS FOR CLASS II PRESCRIBED BY THE NCERT IN ENVIRONMENTAL STUDIES II (GENERAL SCIENCE)

AREA I—MYSELF AND OTHERS

It is completely related to Environmental Studies I (Social Studies).

AREA II—BODY, NUTRITION AND HEALTH

A. HUMAN BODY

1. Revision and extension of Class I work including varied uses of body-parts.

B. PERSONAL HYGIENE

2. Continuation of Class I work.
3. To see relationship between *good health* and *habits of cleanliness*.

C. FOOD AND NUTRITION

4. Extension of Class I work.
5. To associate food with the ability to work and play.
6. Continuation of Class I work.　　　7. Extension of Class I work.

D. CLEANLINESS AND ORDERLINESS

8. Extension of Class I work.
9. Extension of Class I work.
10. Extension of Class I work.

E. SAFETY AND KEEPING HEALTHY

11. Extension of Class I work.

AREA III—THE WORLD AROUND US

A. LIVING THINGS

12. To observe and name various living things in the natural environment.
13. To compare the plants according to *size, shape, colour* etc.
14. Continuation of Class I work.　　　15. Continuation of Class I work.

B. THE MATERIALS

16. To observe various objects in the locality and to state that they are made up of different materials—*glass, metal, wood* etc.

C. THE EARTH, THE SUN, THE MOON

17. Extension of Class I work.
18. Comparing *the sun, the moon* and *stars* in terms of observable features.

AREA IV—TIME AND SPACE

A. SKILLS OF LOCATION
—

B. SKILLS TO USE A GLOBE
—

C. MAP READING SKILLS
—

D. WEATHER/CLIMATE AND ITS INFLUENCE
19. To identify local seasons and their effects on day-to-day life.
20. To identify various types of dresses worn in different seasons.
21. To compare the food-habits of the family with those of other families.

E. ON THE MOVE, REACHING OUT
22. To classify—*slow* and *fast* means of transport.

F. TIME AND DISTANCE
—

G. I AM AN INDIAN.
—

AREA V—NATURAL RESOURCES

A. AIR
23. Extension of Class I work.
24. To list some important uses of *air—breathing, breeze* etc.

B. SOUND
25. To explore ways in which air can create sounds *(whistling, blowing into pipes, playing the flute)* etc.

C. WATER
26. To list some simple uses of water.

D. LAND-FORMS
—

E. ENERGY
—

F. NATURAL RESOURCES
27. Extension of Class I work.

MY BODY AND HEALTH

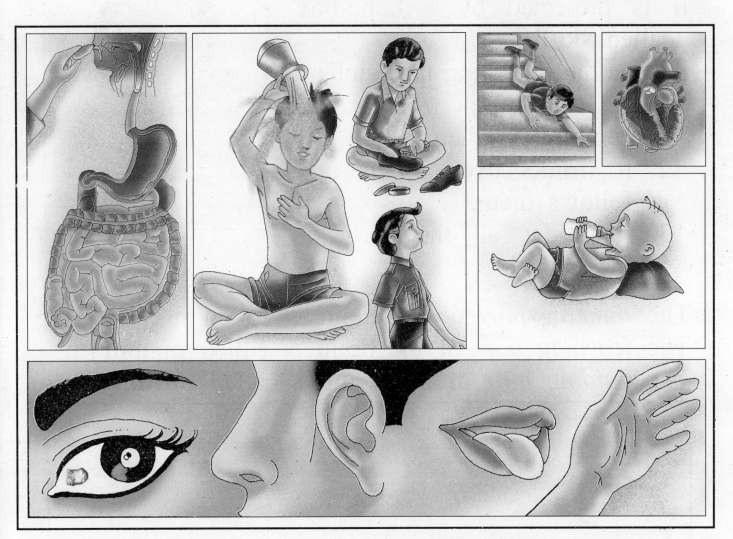

IN THIS UNIT—

1. My Brain
2. My Heart
3. My Lungs
4. My Stomach and Bowels
5. Growing up with Age
6. Clean Habits
7. Safety Habits

1 MY BRAIN

My **brain** is inside my head.
It is protected by a bone-box called **skull**.
It does the following three jobs :

1. It **learns** *new things* and **remembers** them.
2. It **thinks over** *things* and follows them.
3. It **guides** all the parts of the body.

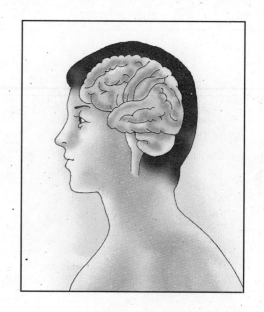

The *thinking part* of the brain is called **mind**.
The *learning part* of the brain is called **memory**.
The *guiding part* of the brain is called **brain centre.**

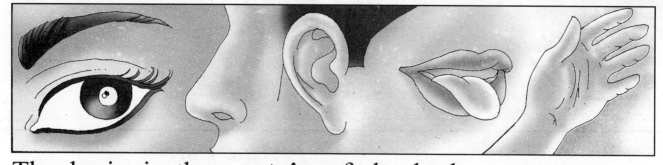

The brain is the **captain** of the body.
All the body-parts obey it.
The sense *organs* also work with its help.

If the brain stops working, a person **goes mad**.
He/She cannot learn and remember anything.
He/She cannot think over things properly.
Other organs of the body do not work properly.

EXERCISES

A. Answer in one word only :

1. Where is your brain located ? ....

2. What protects the brain ? ....

3. What is your brain to your body ? ....

4. How many chief parts are there of the brain ? ....

5. What is the guiding part of the brain called ? ....

B. Colour the picture given in front and complete each sentence :

1. The brain is the .... of the body.

2. Different organs of the body .... the brain.

3. The sense organs work with the .... of the brain.

4. If the brain of a person .... working, he/she goes ....

C. Answer these questions :

1. What is the bone-box protecting the brain called ?

....

2. What does the brain do as the body's captain ?

....

3. What can a mad person not do ?

   1. ....

   2. ....

   3. ....

D. Name the three chief parts of the brain :

....

9

2 MY HEART

My heart is a part of my **trunk**.
It is located in a bone-box called **chest-box**.
It does three main jobs as under :

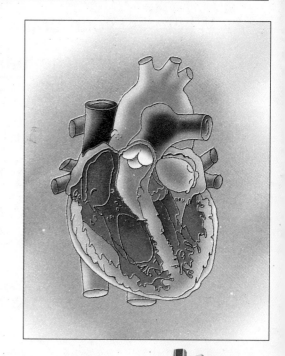

1. It **pumps pure blood** to all parts of the body.
2. It helps me to **feel** in different ways.
3. It **beats non-stop** day and night.

The heart acts as the **engine** of the body.
If the heart fails, the person dies at once.

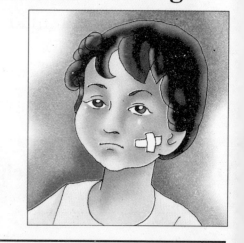

The heart is connected to two lungs.
The lungs send pure blood to the heart.
The heart keeps pumping this blood to all body-parts.
This blood gives energy to the body for work and play.

My feelings have a close link with my heart.
Good events and thoughts lead to **pleasant feelings**.
These feelings make me *happy*.
Bad events and thoughts lead to **unpleasant feelings**.
These feelings make me *sad*.
Desires also take birth in the heart.
The heart is a sensitive organ of the body.

EXERCISES

A. Answer in one word only :

1. What is your heart a part of ? ....

2. Wherein is your heart located ? ....

3. What is the heart closely linked to ? ....

4. What takes birth in the heart ? ....

5. What is the heart connected to ? ....

B. Colour the picture given in front and fill up each blank :

1. My heart .... pure blood to all parts of my body.
2. My heart helps me to .... in different ways.
3. My heart keeps .... non-stop.
4. My heart acts as the .... of my body.
5. My blood gives .... to my body for work and play.

C. Answer these questions :

1. What type of body-organ is the heart ?

....

2. What leads to pleasant feelings ?

....

3. What leads to unpleasant feelings ?

....

4. Wherefrom does pure blood come to the heart ?

....

5. What does the heart act as to my body ?

....

11

3 MY LUNGS

My lungs are inside my trunk.
They are located in the **chest-box**.
They are sensitive organs just like the heart.
One lung is to the right of the heart while the other is to its left.

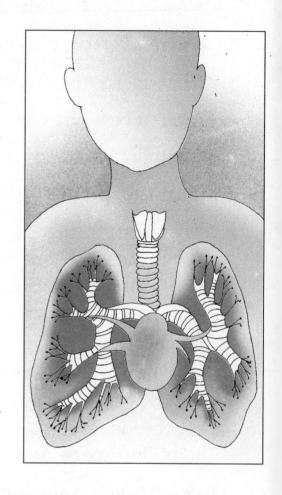

My lungs do three main jobs :
1. They help me to **breathe** fresh air in and out.
2. They use this fresh air to make **my blood pure**.
3. Then they **send this pure blood** to the heart.

The heart gets pure blood from the lungs.
It pumps this blood to all parts of the body.
This blood travels throughout the body.
After this journey, it becomes **dull** and **impure**.
This impure blood returns to the lungs.
The lungs use fresh air on it and **purify** it.
This pure blood is sent to the heart again.
The heart pumps it and it goes on its journey again.
This process goes on non-stop till the end of a person's life.

EXERCISES

A. Answer in one word only :

1 Where are your lungs located ? ....

2. Wherein are your lungs located ? ....

3. Which organ is located between your lungs ? ....

4. What do lungs use to purify blood ? ....

5. Which blood returns to the lungs ? ....

B. Colour the picture given in front and fill up each blank :

1. My lungs help me to .... fresh air in and out.

2. My lungs use fresh air to .... my blood.

3. My lungs send the .... blood to the heart.

4. The pure blood .... throughout my body.

5. The .... blood returns to the lungs.

6. The lungs purify the impure blood with .... air again.

C. Answer these questions :

1. What type of organs are your lungs ?

....

2. What do your lungs help you to do ?

....

3. How do the lungs make impure blood pure ?

....

4. Where do lungs send the pure blood to ?

....

5. Which bone-box protects your lungs ?

....

4 MY STOMACH AND BOWELS

My stomach is in the middle part of my trunk.

It is located in the **top left part of my belly.**

It is **joined to the food-pipe** on its top.

It is **joined to the bowels** at its bottom.

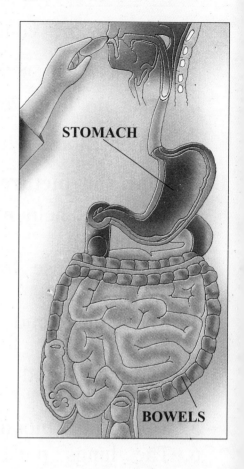

My **stomach** does the following three jobs :

1. It gets **chewed food** from the food-pipe.

2. It **produces some juices** that break up this food.

3. It **churns this food** and sends it to the bowels.

My **bowels** do the following jobs :

They receive the food from the stomach.

They mix it with some more juices.

They digest it fully and it gets mixed with the blood.

This food gives the body energy for work and play.

The undigested food is sent out of the body.

EXERCISES

A. Answer in one word only :

1. Where is your stomach located ? ....

2. What is your stomach joined to at its top ? ....

3. What is your stomach joined to at its bottom ? ....

4. What does the stomach get from the food-pipe ? ....

5. What do the bowels digest fully ? ....

B. Colour the picture given in front and fill up each blank :

1. My bowels .... the food from the stomach.

2. The bowels .... the food with some more juices.

3. The digested food gives .... to the body.

4. The stomach produces some .... that break up the food.

5. The undigested food is sent .... of the body.

C. Answer these questions :

1. In which part of the body is the stomach located ?

....

2. In which part of the belly is the stomach located ?

....

3. How does the body use its energy ?

....

4. What happens to the undigested food ?

....

5 GROWING UP WITH AGE

I am a small child of form II.
I am only six years old.
I was a **baby** when I was born.
I fed on *milk* only at that time.
I could not walk or talk then.

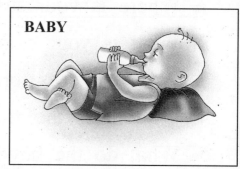

BABY

When I grew up a little, I began to eat other things. This food helped me to grow and I became a **small child**.

SMALL CHILD

LAD   LASS

Now, I eat several things. So, I am growing up day by day. My body is growing in **height, weight** and **girth**. After about 10-12 years, I shall be a **young lad/lass**.

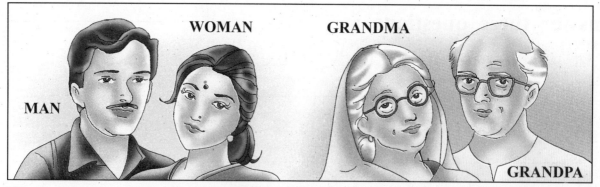

WOMAN   GRANDMA

MAN

GRANDPA

Still later on, I shall grow up into a **young man/woman** just like my *papa/mama*. I shall remain young for many years. Then I shall **grow old** like my **grandpa/grandma**. It is so with everybody indeed.

EXERCISES

A. Answer in one word only :

1. Are you a small boy or girl ? ....

2. How long ago were you a baby ? ....

3. What did you feed on as a baby ? ....

4. How long hence will you be a lad/lass ? ....

5. Does everybody grow with age ? ....

B. Colour each picture and fill up each blank under it :

I was a .... about six years ago.

I shall be a young ..../.......... about 10-12 years hence.

C. Answer these questions :

1. What happens to everybody with age ?

   ....

2. How is your body growing ?

   ....

3. Do you feed on only milk now ?

   ....

4. What does a lad/lass grow into ?

   ....

5. What does a young man/woman grow into ?

   ....

6 CLEAN HABITS

The food helps the body to grow up.

But it is necessary to keep the body safe from disease.

So, I take care of my body in every way.

I observe all the clean habits.

I **have a bath** every morning.

I put on a **clean dress** daily.

I polish **my shoes** every day.

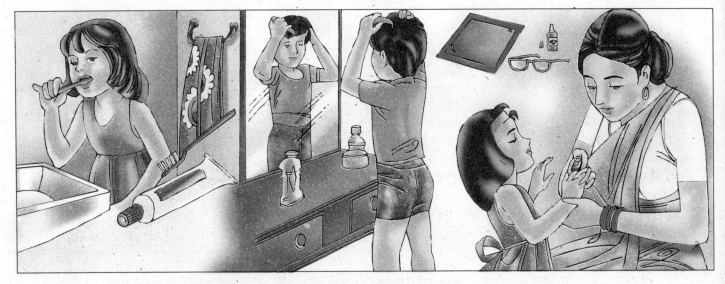

I brush **my teeth** after every meal.

I trim **my nails** regularly.

I also keep my **hair clean**.

I always keep a **hanky** in my pocket.

The air is quite dirty these days. It can trouble my eyes.

So, I put on **goggles** when I go out.

I use an **eye-lotion** also once every day.

EXERCISES

A. Answer in one word only :

1. What helps your body to grow up ? ....

2. From what do you keep your body safe ? ....

3. Which habits do you observe ? ....

4. What do you keep in your pocket always ? ....

5. What do you wear on your eyes ? ....

B. Colour each picture and fill up the blank under it :

I use an .... once every day.

I brush my .... after every meal.

C. Answer these questions :

1. How do you clean your body every day ?

....

2. How do you keep your nails clean ?

....

3. How can dirty air trouble you ?

....

4. What do you do to keep your eyes safe ?

   (a) ....

   (b) ....

7 | SAFETY HABITS

I observe some habits that keep my body quite safe.

I save my body from **bad weather**.

I wear **light clothes** in hot weather.

I wear **woollen clothes** in cold weather.

I use a **rain-coat** when it rains.

I use a **headwear, socks** and **gloves,** when needed.

I always **sit, stand** and **walk upright**. It keeps my body in shape.

I never **tease any pet animal**. It may hurt me.

I never play with **fire** or **sharp** things.

I never **touch a live electric wire**.

I never **run down the stairs**. I may slip and have a bad fall.

EXERCISES

A. Answer in one word only :

1. Which habits do you observe ? ....

2. From what do you save your body ? ....

3. What type of clothes do you wear in summer ? ....

4. What type of clothes do you wear in winter ? ....

5. What do you wear as headwear ? ....

B. Colour each picture and fill up the blank under it :

I always stand and .... upright.

I never tease a .... animal.

C. Answer these questions :

1. How are safety habits useful to you ?

....

2. Which headwear do you wear—a *cap, turban* or *scarf* ?

....

3. In which position do you *sit, stand* and *walk* ?

....

4. Why don't you run down the stairs ?

....

5. How is upright posture useful ?

....

A. Give short answers :

1. What protects your brain ? ....

2. Which part of the brain guides the body ? ....

3. What is heart closely linked to ? ....

4. What leads to unpleasant feelings ? ....

5. What is located between the two lungs ? ....

6. What is the stomach joined to at its bottom ? ....

7. What did you feed on as a baby ? ....

8. Which organ is the *captain* of the body ? ....

9. How do you sit, stand and walk ? ....

10. Which organ is the *engine* of the body ? ....

B. Name—

(a) three parts of the brain :

....

(b) five stages of man's life :

....

C. Answer these questions :

1. What is the bone-box protecting the heart and the lungs called ?

....

2. What type of body organs are the *brain,* the *lungs* and the *heart* ?

....

3. Where is the stomach located in the body ?

....

4. Like whom will you grow old one day ?

....

LIVING AND NON-LIVING THINGS

IN THIS UNIT—

8 | THREE CLASSES OF LIVING THINGS

Living things have life, we know.
Living things fall into three classes :
1. **Human-beings**   2. **Plants**   3. **Animals**

Human-beings include all **men, women** and **children**.
We also use the word—**people**—for human-beings.
Once they were just like other animals.
But slowly they made a lot of progress.
Now they are the top living-beings.
They can **speak very clearly** and **think very deeply**.
They use the *animals* and the *plants* for their good.
Animals are as they were in the past.
They have made no progress at all.
They cannot speak clearly. They can only cry. Nor can
   they think beyond their three basic needs—**food,
   shelter** and **safety**.
Plants can neither *speak* nor *think*.
They cannot *move* from their places either.

EXERCISES

A. Answer in one word only :

1. Into how many classes do living things fall ? ....

2. Which other word is used for human-beings ? ....

3. Which living-beings are the top living-beings ? ....

4. Can plants move about at will ? ....

5. Who are using the animals and the plants for their good ?.....

B. Colour each picture and fill up the blank under it :

.... include men, women and children.

Animals can think of food, shelter and .... only.

C. Answer these questions :

1. How were the human-beings in early times ?

....

2. What has made human-beings the top living-beings ?

....

3. In what way do animals speak ?

....

4. Which three things can plants not do ?

....

5. What do human-beings include ?

....

9 THE LOCAL ENVIRONMENT

The word—**environment**—means *surroundings*.
It means the **land** and **water** around a place.
It means **heat** and **cold** at a place.
It means **food-supply** at a place.
It means the **plants, animals** and **people** at a place.

Look at the picture given above. It shows the environment of a house.
Its environment shows two types of things.
Living things include people, animals and plants.
Non-living things include *land, water, heat* and *cold*. In one word, they are called **weather**.
So, environment has two types of things—**living** and **non-living**.
Life at a place depends on its environment.

EXERCISES

A. Answer in one word only :

1 What does the word—*environment*—mean ? ....

2. What type of things are *people, plants* and *animals* ? ....

3. What type of things are *land, water, heat* and *cold* ? ....

4. What does life at a place depend on ? ....

B. Colour this picture.

C. Answer these questions :

1. What are *heat, cold, land* and *water* at a place called ?

....

2. What depends on the environment at a place ?

....

3. What do living things at a place include ?

....

4. What do non-living things at a place include ?

....

5. What does the food-supply at a place include ?

....

10 ANIMALS ARE USEFUL TO US.

We keep several animals.
They are useful to us in many
different ways.

A. MILCH ANIMALS
These animals give us milk.
They include the **cow,** the **yak,**
the **goat** and the **buffalo.**

B. PACK ANIMALS
Pack animals carry our loads on their backs.
They also give us rides. They include the **ass,** the
mule, the **horse,** the **camel** and the **yak.**

Pack animals

Draught animals

C. DRAUGHT ANIMALS
These animals draw loaded vehicles for us.
They include **oxen, he-buffaloes, camels** and **horses.**
Horses draw *tongas* for us.

D. FARM ANIMALS

These animals work on our farms. They include **oxen, he-buffaloes** and **camels**.
They draw our ploughs and carts.
They work our wells also.

E. MEAT AND EGGS

Hens, ducks and **geese** lay eggs for us.
Sheep, he-goats and **cocks** are kept for meat.

F. OTHER USEFUL THINGS

Sheep give us *wool* for our *winter clothes*.
Hair of **horses** is used to make *brushes*.
Hair of camel is used to make *blankets*.
Dead **animals** give us *hides* and *bones*.
Hides are made into **leather**.
Leather is used to make *shoes, belts, bags* and *purses*.
Bones are used to make *combs, needles* and *ornaments*.
They are used to make *handles of things* as well.

EXERCISES

A. Answer in one word only :

1. Which animals give us milk ? ....

2. Which animals carry loads on their backs ? ....

3. Which animals draw loaded vehicles ? ....

4. What do hens and ducks give us ? ....

5. What are cocks and he-goats kept for ? ....

6. Which two things do dead animals give us ? ....

B. Colour each picture and fill up the blank under it :

Shoes and purses are made of

....

Bones are used to make ....
and needles.

C. Answer these questions :

1. How is hair of horses used ?

....

2. How is hair of camels used ?

....

3. What are hides of dead animals made into ?

....

4. Which three animals are kept for meat ?

....

5. What do we use *wool* for ?

....

30

11 PLANTS ARE USEFUL TO US.

Plants are also useful to us in many ways.
We get several useful things from plants.

A. SHADE AND WOOD

Plants give us **cool shade** in the sun.
We rest in the shade in summer.
Plants also give us useful wood.
It is used to make *furniture, sports goods, doors* and *windows*. It is also used as *fuel*.

B. CORN, PULSES, FODDER

Plants give us various types of corn—*wheat, rice, maize* etc.
They give us various **pulses** as well.
They give us *green fodder* for our domestic animals.

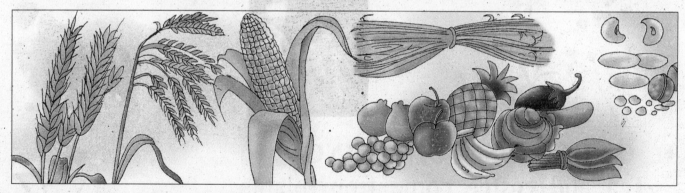

C. FRUITS, VEGETABLES, SPICES

Plants give us **green juicy fruits.**
They give us **dry fruit**—*almonds, walnuts, pea-nuts.*

Plants give us **green vegetables** and **salads**.

They also give us **green spices**—*chillies, garlic, onion, mint* etc.

They give us **dry spices**—*pepper, cardamom, cloves, turmeric, coriander* etc.

D. FIBRES

Plants give us fibres for cloth and various other things.

Cotton fibre is used to make *cloth*.

Jute fibre is used to make *gunny bags*.

Flax and **hemp fibres** are used to make ropes.

Coconut coir is used to make **mats** and **carpets**.

COTTON

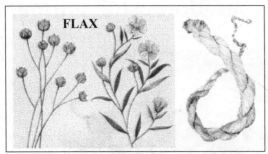

FLAX

TEA

COFFEE

CORIANDER

PEPPER

E. OTHER USEFUL THINGS

Tea and **coffee** come from plants.

Latex of a plant is used to make **rubber**.

Several **herb-plants** are used as **medicines**.

Flowers-plants give us beautiful **flowers**.

EXERCISES

A. Answer in one word only :

1. What do plants give us for summer ? ....

2. How do we use wood in the kitchen ? ....

3. What are wheat, rice and maize called ? ....

4. What are almonds, walnuts and pea-nuts called ? ....

5. What do we make from cotton fibre ? ....

B. Name—

(a) four green spices : ....

(b) four dry spices : ....

(c) four green vegetables : ....

(d) four green fruits : ....

(e) four fibre plants : ....

B. Colour each picture and fill up the blank under it :

These are .... plants.   These are .... plants.

C. Answer these questions :

1. What are ropes and gunny bags made of ?

....

2. Which plant gives us fibre for cloth ?

....

3. Is *maize* a type of *corn* or *pulse* ?

....

4. What do we use green fodder for ?

....

12 CARE OF THE ANIMALS

Animals are so useful to us.
So, we must care for them in every
way.
We must feed them with **good food**.
We must provide them with **clean
water** to drink.
We must provide them with **clean and cosy shelter**.

We must keep their bodies clean.
Body-lice often grow on their bodies.
We must remove them because they suck their blood.
We must give **good baths** to our buffaloes in summer.
We must **brush the bodies** of our horses properly.

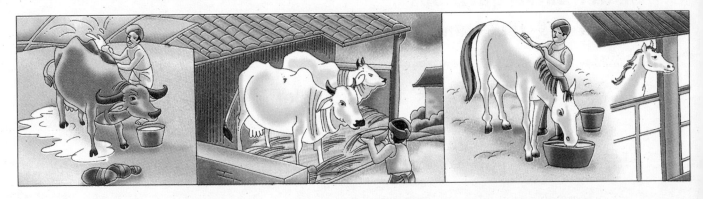

If we look after our animals well, they will love us.
Also they will serve us in a much better way.

EXERCISES

A. Answer in one word only :

1. Which insect sucks the blood of animals ? ....

2. What type of water should we give to our animals ....

3. Which animal needs a good bath in summer ? ....

4. Which animal needs brushing of its body ? ....

5. What should we feed our animals with ? ....

B. Colour each picture and fill up the blank under it :

We must give good .... to our buffaloes in summer.

We must .... the bodies of our horses properly.

C. Answer these questions :

1. How should we care for our animals ?

....

2. What type of shelter should be given to animals ?

....

3. How do body-lice harm our animals ?

....

4. When will our animals love us ?

....

5. How will well-cared-for animals show their love for us ?

....

35

13 CARE OF THE PLANTS

Plants are useful to us in many ways.
They are the **chief source of food** for all animals and human-beings.
They help in **bringing rain** and keep the air fresh.
They also **prevent floods** and **save our fertile soil.**
So, we must look after them carefully.
We must water our crops and flower-pots in time.
We must also feed them with good manure.

We must save them from stray animals.
Strong fences should be put up round the crop-fields.
We must spray our crops with chemicals that kill harmful insects.
We must not cut trees and useful plants aimlessly.
We must grow new plants regularly.

EXERCISES

A. Answer in one word only :

1. What are plants the chief source of ?   ....

2. What must we feed the plants with ?   ....

3. What must we save the plants from ?   ....

4. What should be put up round crop-fields ?   ....

5. What do plants prevent ?   ....

B. Colour each picture and fill up the blank under it :

Plants help in bringing ....   We must .... new plants.

C. Answer these questions :

1. When should we water our crops and flower-pots ?

....

2. How can we save our crops from stray animals ?

....

3. How can we save our crops from harmful insects ?

....

4. Which soil do plants save ?

....

5. What do plants keep fresh for us ?

....

14 PARTS OF A PLANT

Look at the picture given in front. It shows a plant.

A plant has six chief parts :
1. Roots   2. Stem
3. Branches 4. Leaves
5. Flowers   6. Fruit

Roots of a plant are under the soil. They suck water for it from the soil. They send this water to its upper parts.

The **trunk** of a plant is its thickest part.

It gets water from the roots and sends it to the branches.

The **branches** of a plant spread out in all directions.

The leaves grow on branches. The leaves give the plant an umbrella-like shape.

The **flowers** grow out of buds. They further grow into fruits.

Most plants grow from seeds.

They need **air, water** and **sunlight** to grow well.

EXERCISES

A. Answer in one word only :

1. How many parts are there of a plant ? ....

2. Which part of a plant is under the soil ? ....

3. Where do leaves of a plant grow ? ....

4. What do flowers grow out of ? ....

5. What do flowers grow into ? ....

B. Colour each picture and fill up the blank under it :

Most plants .... from seeds.

The .... is the thickest part of a plant.

C. Answer these questions :

1. How many parts of a plant are above the soil ?

....

2. What do roots suck from under the soil for the plant ?

....

3. How do branches of a plant spread out ?

....

4. What do plants need to grow well ?

....

5. What do most plants grow from ?

....

15 | NON-LIVING THINGS

Non-living things are *lifeless* things.
They are quite different from living things.
They are not born ; nor do they grow.
They do not eat food ; nor do they drink water.
They cannot move at will like living-things.
They do not grow young ; nor do they die.

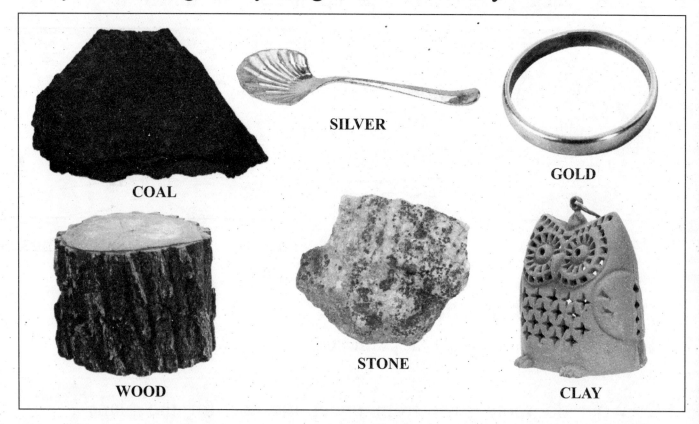

SILVER

GOLD

COAL

WOOD

STONE

CLAY

Non-living things do not bear any young-ones either.
They wear out due to the effect of weather.
They include different materials.
We use these materials to make different articles of use.
Non-living things include **wood, stone, coal, clay, silver, gold** etc. These non-living things are **natural materials**.

But man has made a number of other materials also.
They are also non-living things.
They are called **man-made materials**.
They include **iron, steel, brass, plastics, glass, plywood, cement, cloth, silk, nylon** and many other materials.

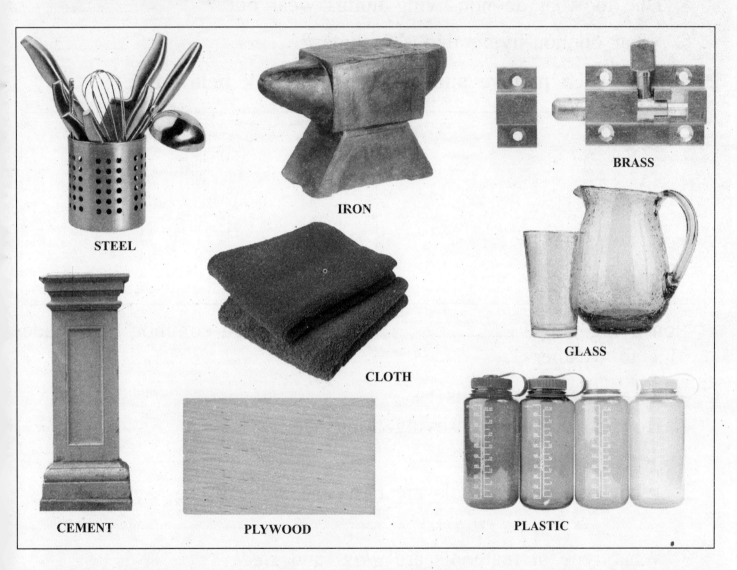

STEEL

IRON

BRASS

CLOTH

GLASS

CEMENT

PLYWOOD

PLASTIC

The pictures given above show several man-made materials.
These materials are also very, very useful to us.
We use them to make different things of daily use.
We cannot do without them in the world of today.

EXERCISES

A. Answer in one word only :

1. What are non-living things ? ....

2. Are non-living things like living things ? ....

3. Do non-living things grow up ? ....

4. Due to what do non-living things wear out ? ....

5. What do non-living things include ? ....

B. Colour each picture and fill up the blank below it :

Non-living things .... due to weather.

Plastics is a common man-made ....

C. Answer these questions :

1. How do we use non-living things ?

....

2. What type of materials are *clay* and *stone* ?

....

3. What type of materials are *glass* and *steel* ?

....

4. Can we do without non-living things ?

....

5. What are materials made by man called ?

....

REVISION–II

A. Give short answers :

1. How many classes are there of living things ? ....

2. Which other word is used for human-beings ? ....

3. What does life at a place depend on ? ....

4. What does the word—*environment*—mean ? ....

5. Which animals carry loads on their backs ? ....

6. What are cocks and he-goats kept for ? ....

7. What are wheat, rice and maize called ? ....

8. How do we use wood in the kitchen ? ....

9. What do we make from cotton-fibre ? ....

10. Which insect sucks the blood of animals ? ....

11. What are plants the chief source of ? ....

12. Which part of a plant is under the soil ? ....

B. What does each picture show ?

....

....

....

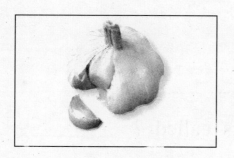
....

....

....

C. Answer these questions :

1. How do body-lice harm our animals ?

....

2. How do well-cared-for animals show their love for us ?

....

3. How can we save our crops from stray animals ?

....

4. How can we save our crops from harmful insects ?

....

5. What do most plants grow from ?

....

6. What type of materials are *wood* and *gold* ?

....

7. What type of materials are *plastics* and *nylon* ?

....

8. Which three things can plants not do ?

....

9. What are hides of dead animals made into ?

....

10. For which two things are sheep kept ?

....

11. What is jute-fibre used for ?

....

12. What are almonds, walnuts and pea-nuts called ?

....

THE EARTH AND THE SKY

IN THIS UNIT—

16 THE SKY AND THE SUN

Go out in the open and look above your head.
You will see a dome of light blue colour.
What is this *dome ?* It is the **sky**.

What is the **sky** ? Can you tell ?
It is nothing but **empty space**.
The sky has no end anywhere.

We see many things in the sky.
We see the **sun** shining in the sky by day.
Sometimes, we see **clouds** and the **rainbow** also.
We see the **moon** and the **stars** at night.

THE SUN

The sun is a big ball of hot gases.
It gives out flames that emit rays in all directions.
The hot sun-rays carry **heat** and **light** with them.
The sun looks rising in the **east** in the *morning*.

It looks just overhead at *noon*.
It looks setting in the **west** in the *evening*.

Sunlight is a boon for the Earth.
She is full of living things due to sunlight only.
The sun is the chief source of **heat** and **light**.
It is the chief source of **energy** as well.

But for the sun, there would be dark everywhere.
There would be no living thing either anywhere.

EXERCISES

A. Answer in one word only :

1. What is the sky ? ....

2. Where is the end of the sky ? ....

3. What do we see shining in the sky by day ? ....

4. When do we see the stars in the sky ? ....

5. Are the sun-rays cold or hot ? ....

B. Colour each picture and fill up the blank under it :

Sometimes we see .... in the sky.

Sunlight is a .... for the Earth.

C. Answer these questions :

1. What is the sun ?

    ....

2. What do sun-rays carry ?

    ....

3. How is sunlight a boon for the earth ?

    ....

4. Where does the sun look at noon ?

    ....

5. Which three things is the sun chief source of ?

    ....

17 THE MOON AND THE STARS

Look at the sky on a clear night.
It looks full of stars all over.
These stars are countless indeed.
They twinkle like small lamps.
They are all hot like the sun.
The stars are there by day as well.
But we cannot see them in bright sunlight.
The heat of the stars does not reach our earth.
Because they are far, far away from it.
The sun is also a star. It is the nearest star to the earth.

The moon is also there in the sky every night.
It appears in a new *form* and *size* every night.
The **full moon** is there once a month.
But **half moon** occurs twice a month.
Moonlight is *cool* and *pleasant*.

EXERCISES

A. Answer in one word only :

1. When do stars appear in the sky ? ....

2. How many stars are there in the sky ? ....

3 Are the stars hot or cold bodies? ....

4. Are the stars there by day also ? ....

5. Is moonlight cool or hot ? ....

6. How often does *half-moon* occur every month ? ....

B. Colour each picture and fill up the blank under it :

The full moon occurs .... a month.

The stars .... like small lamps.

C. Answer these questions :

1. How do stars twinkle ?

....

2. How does the moon appear every day ?

....

3. How often does the *full moon* occur every month ?

....

4. Why doesn't the *star-heat* reach us ?

....

5. Why can't we see the stars by day ?

....

50

18 SOME FEATURES OF THE AIR

Air is all about us. It is our primary need. We breathe it in and out all the time. But it has **some features**. They are as under :

1. AIR TAKES UP SPACE.

Air is a mixture of some gases.

So, it takes up space like other things.

Take two balloons of the same size.

Blow air into one of them.

It will become almost round.

What has made it so ?

It is air that has **taken up the space** inside the balloon.

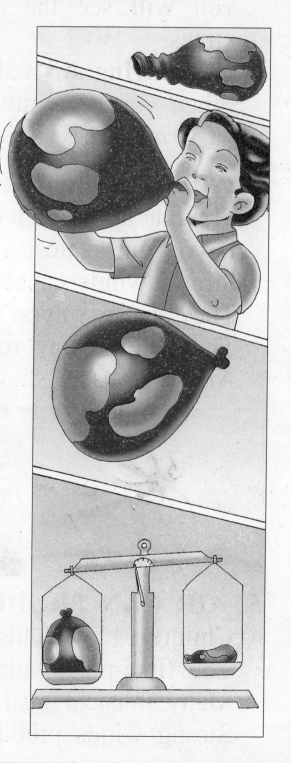

2. AIR HAS WEIGHT.

Air has weight like many other things.

Weigh the balloons of the above experiment.

Weigh them against each other.

The balloon with air in it will be *heavier.* Clearly, air **has weight**.

3. AIR CAN MOVE.

We cannot see the air because it is colourless.

Look out of the window of your room.

You will see the *moving twigs* of trees.

The **moving air** makes them move.

When your mummy washes clothes, she hangs them on a string. They move to and fro with the **moving air**.

4. AIR HAS FORCE.

Moving air is called **wind**. It has force in it.

If you run against a wind, it will try to push you back.

Strong winds cause the dust to rise.

They cause waves in water.

They blow away roofs of huts and uproot trees.

All these facts show that **air has force**.

5. AIR CAN PRODUCE SOUND.

Children blow whistles using their breath.

The flute-player plays on the flute with his breath.

Many musical instruments work using the air.

Strong winds produce sounds when they blow.

EXERCISES

A. Answer in one word only :

1 Where is the air ? ....

2. What do we use air for all the time ? ....

3. What is moving air called ? ....

4. What does air take up ? ....

5. What can air produce ? ....

6. What colour is the air ? ....

B. Colour each picture and fill up the blank under it :

Strong winds cause the .... to rise.

Children blow .... using the breath.

C. Answer these questions :

1. What is air a mixture of ?

....

2. Which balloon is the heavier—empty or inflated ?

....

3. What makes the clothes hanging on a string move ?

....

4. What do strong winds produce when they blow ?

....

5. What is meant by *wind* ?

....

19 THREE STATES OF WATER

Water is our primary need.
We drink it when thirsty.
We use it in several ways.
Water has three forms/states.

Normal water is **liquid water**.
We use it in different ways.
It is there in **water-bodies**.
It is there in **wells** and **springs**.
We get it from **hand-pumps** and **taps**.

Frozen water is **ice** or **snow**.
We use *ice* in cold drinks.
Snow falls on high mountains.
Ice/snow is lighter than water.
Water becomes a gas when it is heated.
This gas is called **vapour**.
It is also lighter than water.
Thus we see that water has three forms/states.
They are *liquid water, ice* and *vapour*.

EXERCISES

A. Answer in one word only :

1. How many states does water have ? ....

2. Where do we find liquid water ? ....

3. Which form of water do we use in cold drinks ? ....

4. Where does snow fall ? ....

5. Where does water-vapour go ? ....

B. Colour each picture and fill up the blank under it :

.... water is called ice or snow.

Gas-like form of water is called ....

C. Answer these questions :

1. How do we use ice ?

....

2. Is ice/snow heavier or lighter than water ?

....

3. Is vapour lighter or heavier than water ?

....

4. When does water change into vapour ?

....

5. What is the normal form of water called ?

....

55

20 DAY AND NIGHT

The sun is in the sky, we know.
The sun is a ball of hot gases.
Its flames emit hot rays.
These rays carry *light* with them.
They carry light to all parts of the sky.

The earth is also in the sky, we know.
So, the rays of the sun fall on it as well.

The earth is round in shape like an orange.
So, only half the earth becomes bright with sunlight.
This bright half of the earth has **day.**
The other half of the earth does not get any sunlight.
So, it remains dark and has **night.**

EXERCISES

A. Answer in one word only :

1. Where is the sun located ? ....

2. What do flames of the sun emit ? ....

3. What do sun-rays carry with them ? ....

4. Where is the earth located ? ....

5. What shape is our earth ? ....

B. Colour each picture and fill up the blank under it :

The flames of the sun .... hot rays.

The rays of the sun fall on the .... too.

C. Answer these questions :

1. What do sun-rays carry with them ?

....

2. Like what is the earth round ?

....

3. How much of the earth becomes bright with sunlight ?

....

4. What is there in the bright half of the earth ?

....

5. What is there in the dark half of the earth ?

....

21 THE SEASONS

A **season** is the total of the weather of several months.
We have **five seasons** during the year.

1. SUMMER SEASON

This season starts in the middle of April.
It goes upto the middle of July.
It is **very hot** during this season.
Days are very long but nights are short.
A **hot wind** blows during the day.

2. RAINY SEASON

This season starts in the middle of July.
It goes on upto the middle of September.
The sky is mostly covered with clouds.
It rains again and again—sometimes very heavily.
So, there is water and water everywhere.

3. AUTUMN SEASON

This season starts in the middle of September.
It goes on upto the middle of November.
The rains are over and the weather is dry.
It is neither very hot nor very cold.
Leaves of trees turn yellow and get ready to fall off.

4. WINTER SEASON

This season starts in mid-November.
It goes on upto mid-February.
It is very cold during this season.
Icy winds blow and dense fog is there.
Leaves of trees fall off leaving them bare.

5. SPRING SEASON

This season starts in February.
It goes up to the middle of April.
It is pleasant in this season.
Trees bring forth new leaves.
Beautiful flowers bloom everywhere.
Everyone feels light, fresh and gay.
This season is the **queen of seasons**.
After this season, the summer season starts again.

EXERCISES

A. Answer in one word only :

1. How many seasons are there in all ? ....

2. Which season lasts from July to September ? ....

3. During which season does a hot wind blow ? ....

4. During which season do tree-leaves turn yellow ? ....

5. Which season is the queen of seasons ? ....

B. Colour each picture and fill up the blank under it :

Leaves of trees fall off during .... season.

The sky is covered with .... during the rainy season.

C. Answer these questions :

1. Which season follows the rainy season ?

....

2. Which season is the most pleasant of all the seasons ?

....

3. During which season do icy cold winds blow ?

....

4. During which season do tree-leaves fall off ?

....

5. Why is spring season called the *queen of seasons* ?

....

22 SEASONS AFFECT LIFE.

Seasons affect our day-to-day life.
They affect our **food** and **dress**.
They affect our **day-to-day** work.

A. The **summer season** is a very hot season.
We wear light clothes.
We have cold drinks again and again.
We use **fans** and **coolers** to beat the heat.
We sleep in the open or on roofs at night.

B. The **rainy season** is a very wet season.
It keeps raining most of the time.
So, we use **rain-coats** and **umbrellas**.
We also sweat very heavily.
Green grass grows everywhere.
Poodles are full of rain-water.
Washermen are not able to dry up their wash.

C. The **autumn season** is a dry season.
Dry winds blow and turn the tree-leaves yellow.

It is neither very hot nor very cold.

So, people wear normal clothes.

Farmers plough fields for the winter crops.

D. The **winter season** is a very cold season.

We wear woollen clothes to beat the cold.

We have hot drinks again and again.

We use room-heaters, and make **bon-fires**.

We sleep **indoors** at night to be safe from the cold.

We use **mattresses**, **quilts** and **blankets**.

Farmers sow winter crops.

E. The **spring season** is a very pleasant season.

People have walks in parks and gardens.

They look fresh and gay.

The crops in fields are about to ripen.

They look golden yellow.

Beautiful flowers bloom everywhere on plants.

Butterflies and **bees** hover around them and suck their *nectar*.

EXERCISES

A. Answer in one word only :

1. How do main seasons affect us ? ....

2. During which season do we use rain-coats ? ....

3. During which season do we use fans and coolers ? ....

4. During which season do we use room-heaters ? ....

5. Which season is a very dry season ? ....

B. Colour each picture and fill up the blank under it :

Dry winds turn the leaves .... in autumn.

Bees hover around .... in spring.

C. Answer these questions :

1. Which three things do seasons affect chiefly ?

....

2. During which season do we sleep indoors ?

....

3. During which season do we use quilts ?

....

4. During which season do washermen suffer ?

....

5. During which season do farmers prepare fields for winter crops ?

....

REVISION–III

A. Give short answers :

1. What is the sky ? ....

2. What do sun-rays carry ? ....

3. Is moonshine moon's own light ? ....

4. Are the stars hot or cold bodies ? ....

5. What is moving air called ? ....

6. What colour is the air ? ....

7. Where is the earth located ? ....

8. What shape is our earth ? ....

9. When does a hot wind blow ? ....

10. Whose work suffers in the rainy season ? ....

11. Which season is the *queen of seasons* ? ....

B. Answer these questions :

1. What is frozen water called ?

   ....

2. What is gas-like form of water called ?

   ....

3. Where does water-vapour go ?

   ....

4. Is ice lighter or heavier than water ?

   ....

5. Is water-vapour lighter or heavier than water

   ....

6. How often does the full-moon occur every month ?

   ....